ABOUT THE AUTHOR

Will Braid is an author and graphic designer that seeks to grow his portfolio of designs and self publish more books in the future.

30 Days Affirmations Coloring Book

WILL BRAID

ISBN: 1532741324
ISBN-13: 978-1532741326

DEDICATION

To every person that has a three year old within themselves looking to enjoy the simplest activity of coloring an image.

CONTENTS

Title | Pg

1 When You Feel Lonely and Sad — 6

2 When You Feel Terrified — 12

3 When You Feel Insignificant — 19

4 When You Are Nervous or Afraid — 25

5 When You Are Angry — 31

6 When You Feel Hopeless — 38

7 When You Feel Conflicted — 45

8 Acknowledgements — 50

9 Notes — 51

10 Index — 52

1 WHEN YOU FEEL LONELY AND SAD

test coloring page

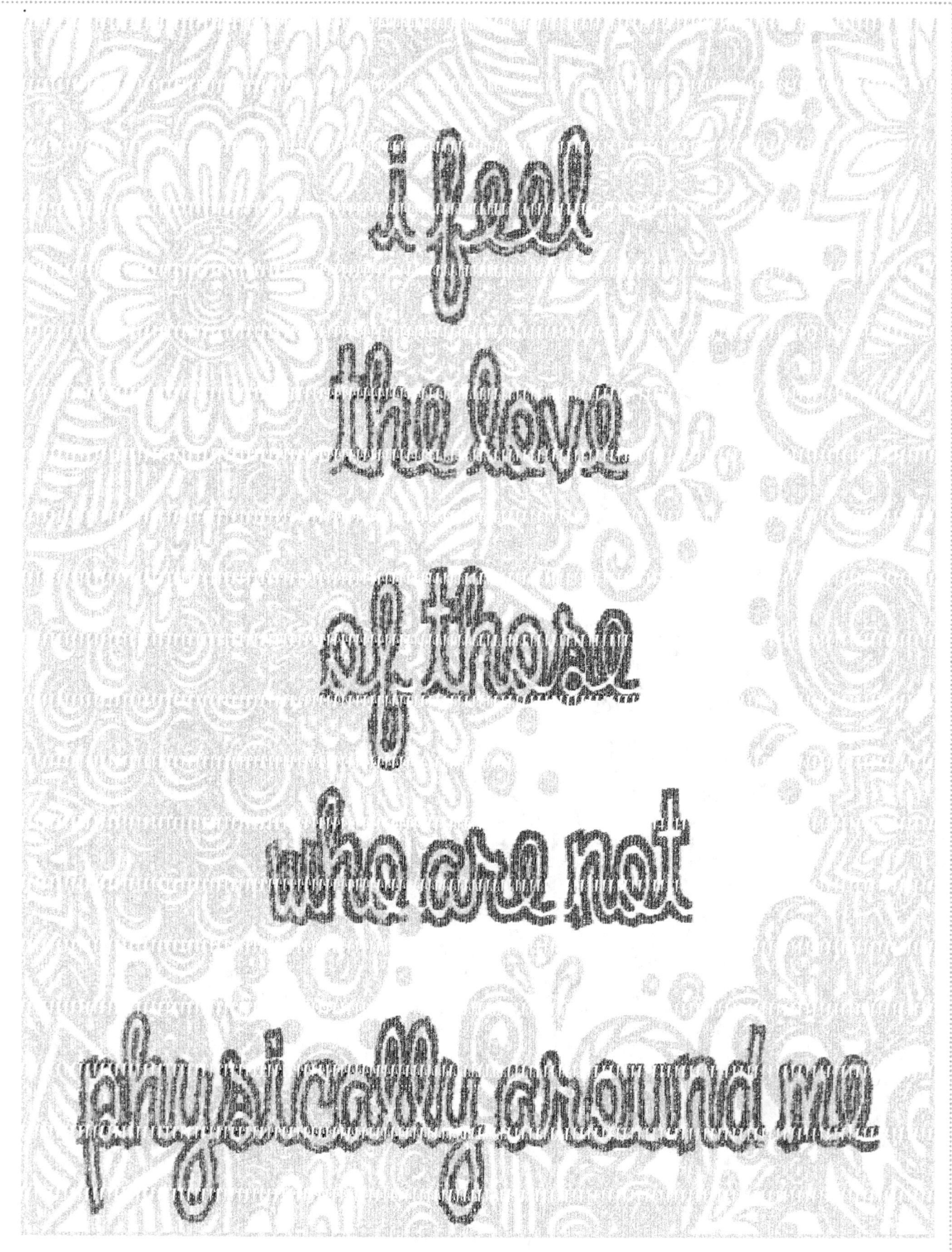

i feel
the love
of those
who are not
physically around me

i take
pleasure
in
my
own
solitude

i am too big

of a gift

to this world

to feel

self pity

my own

solitude

2 WHEN YOU FEEL TERRIFIED

test coloring page

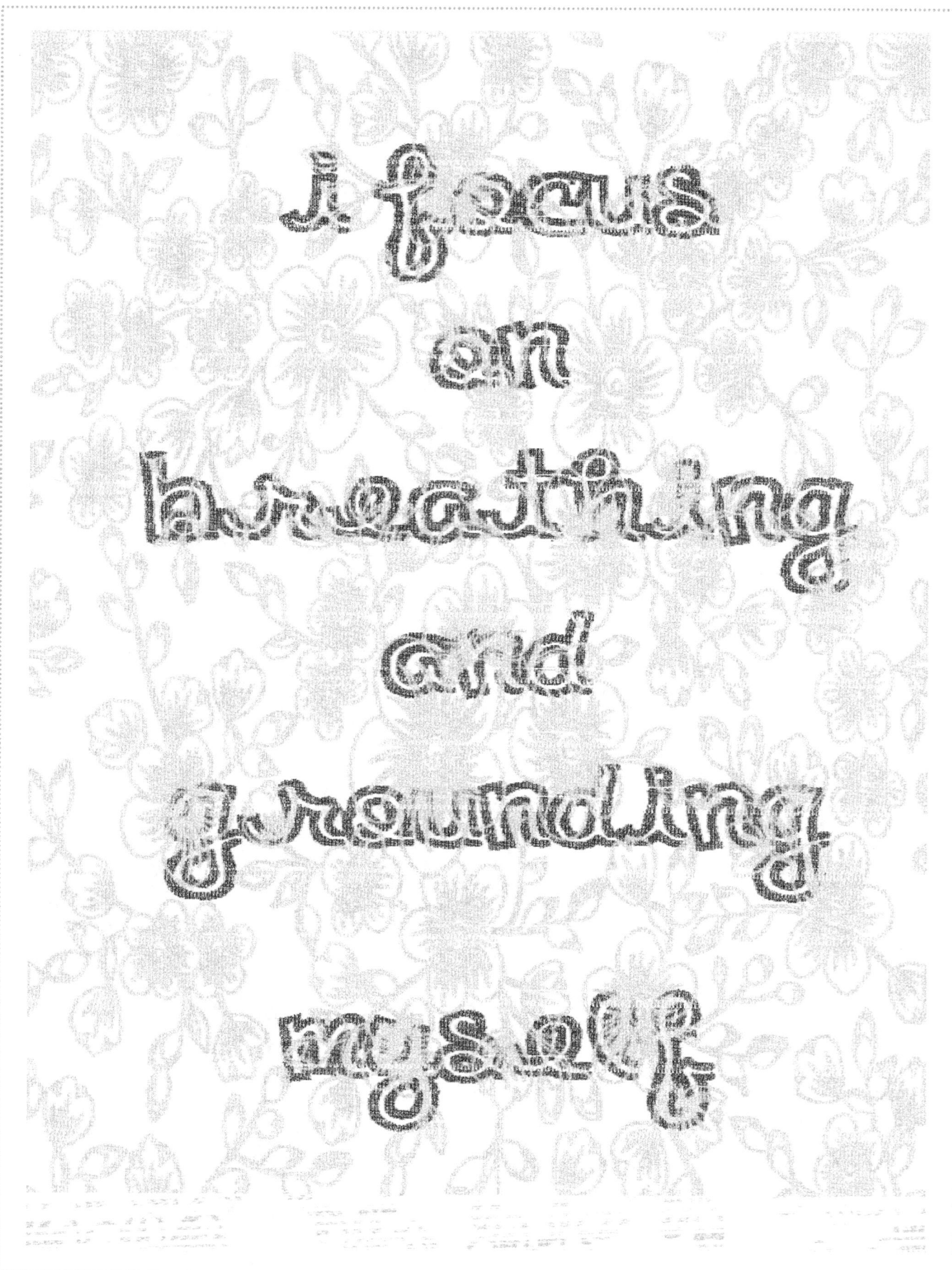

i focus on breathing and grounding myself

follow my intuition and my heart keeps me safe and sound

i make the right choices every time

i draw from my inner strength and light

3 WHEN YOU FEEL INSIGNIFICANT

test coloring page

i matter
and what
i have to offer
this world
also matters.

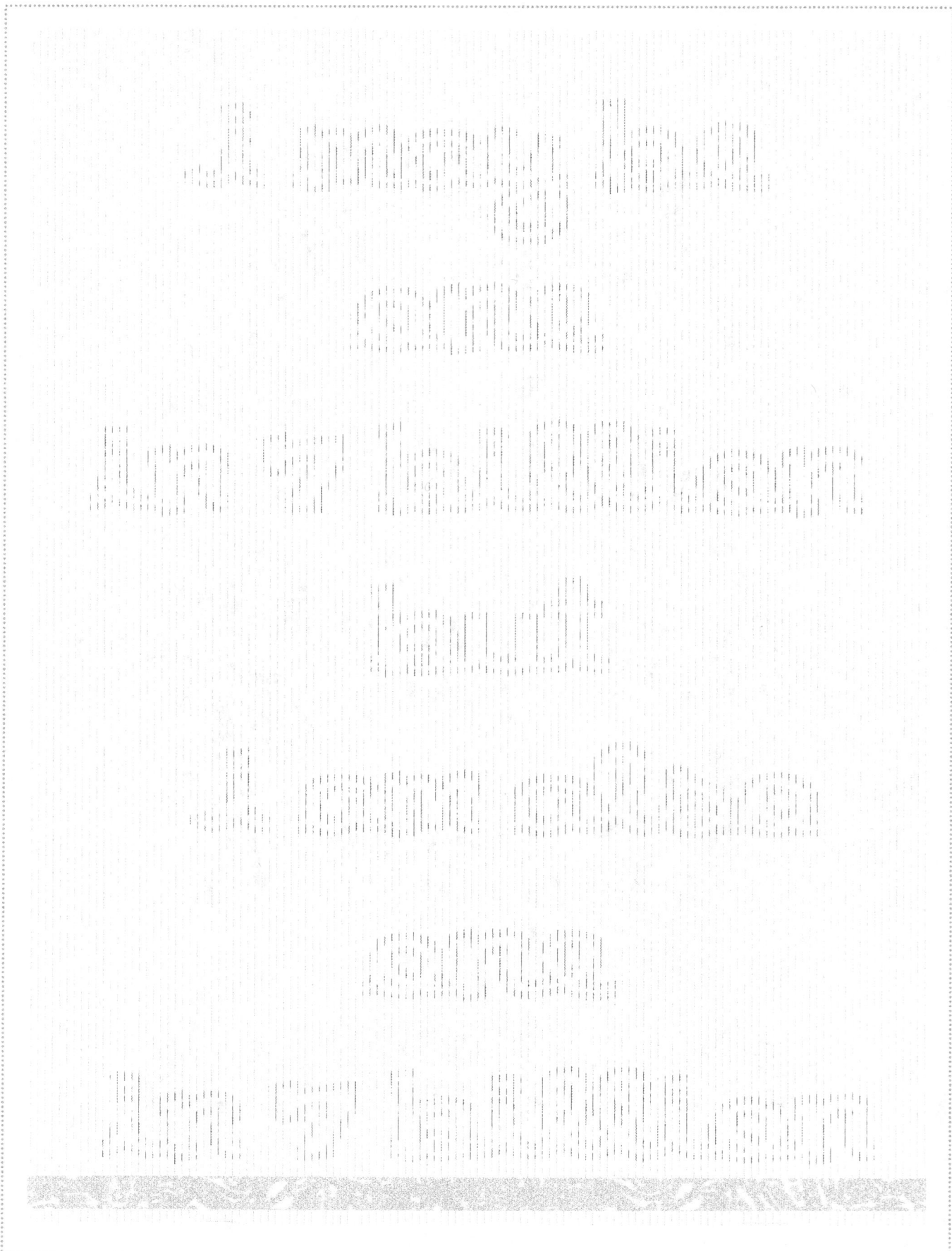

4 WHEN YOU ARE NERVOUS OR AFRAID

test coloring page

I trust my inner wisdom and intuition

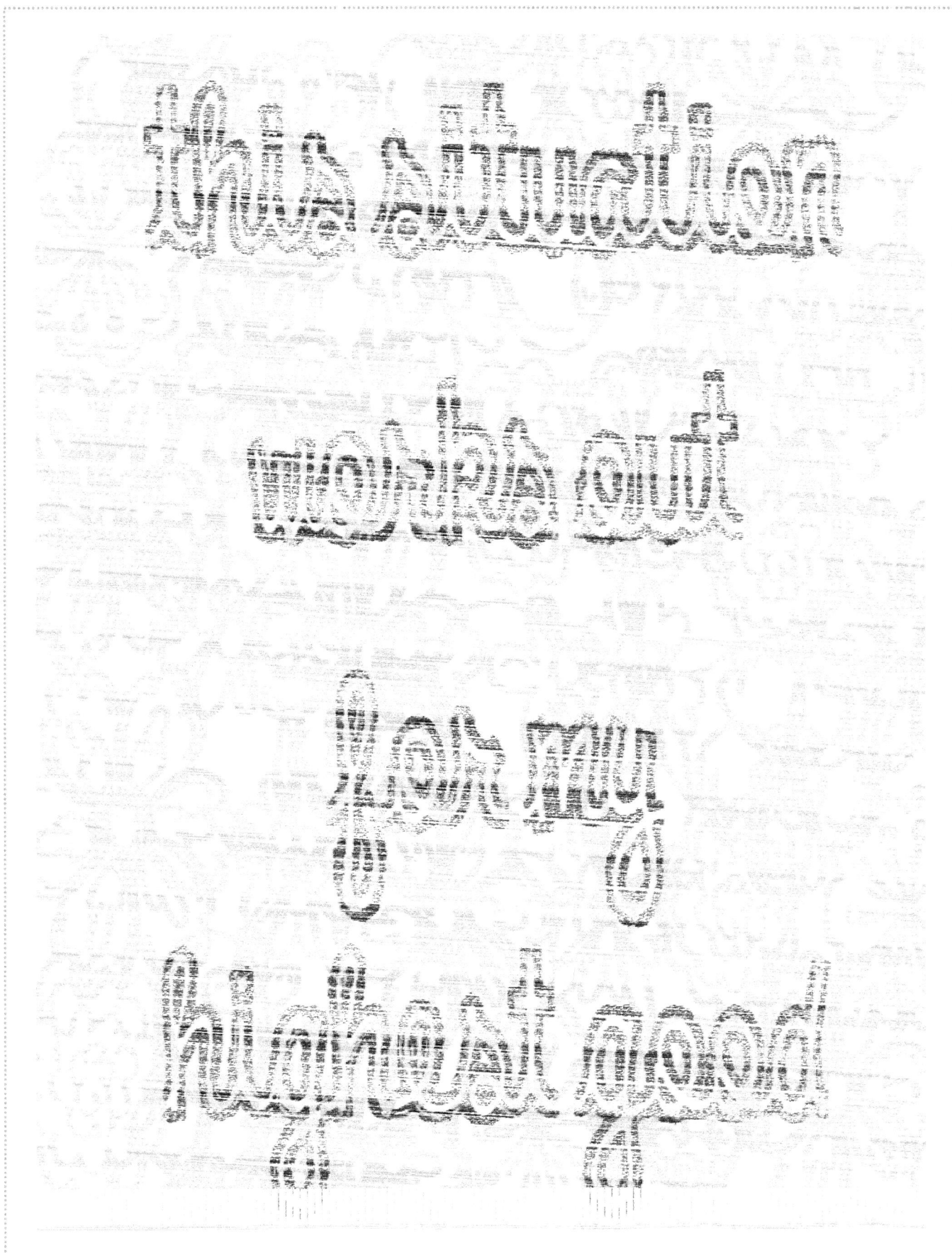

this situation
working out
for my
highest good

wonderful
things
unfold
before
me

5 WHEN YOU ARE ANGRY

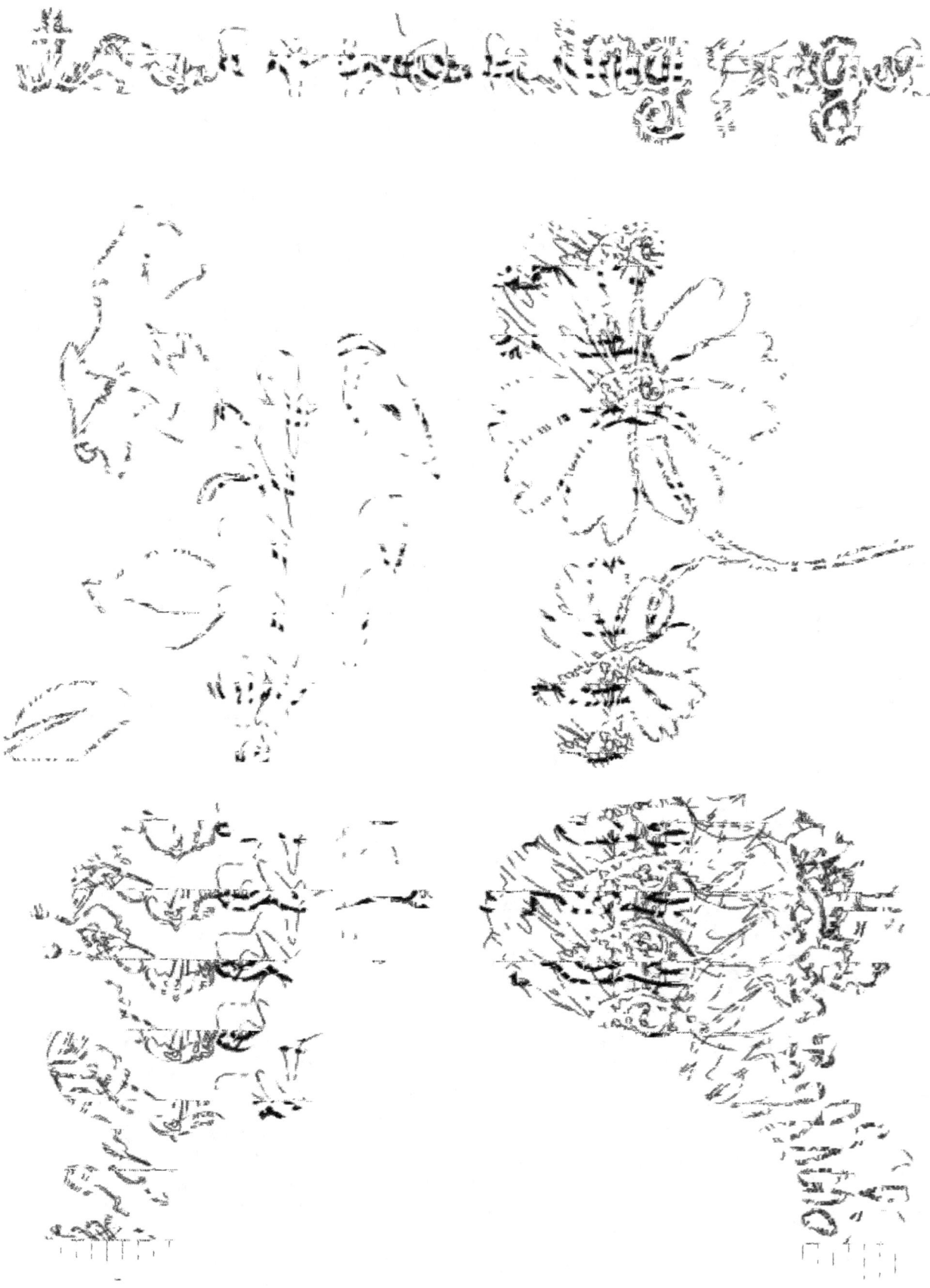

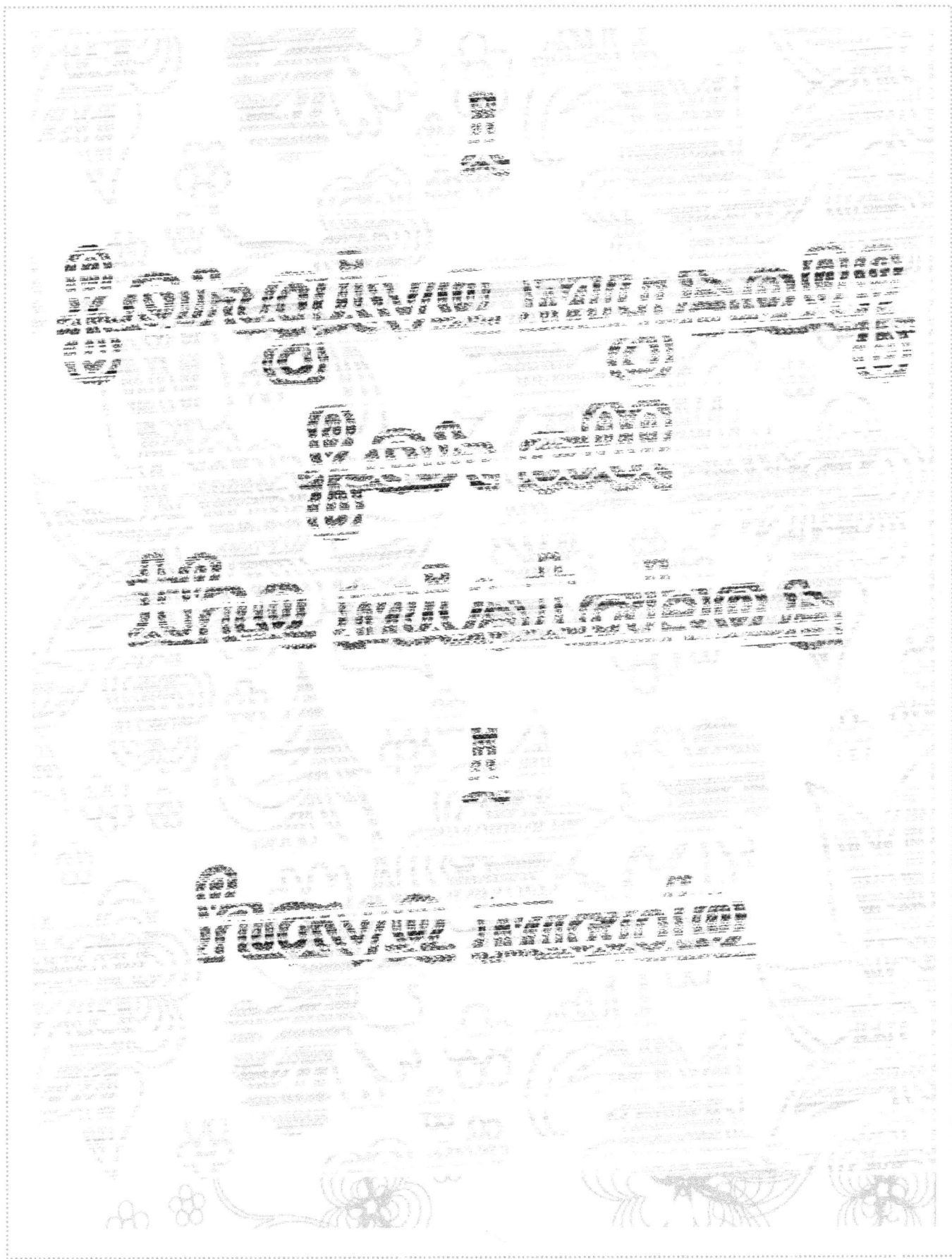

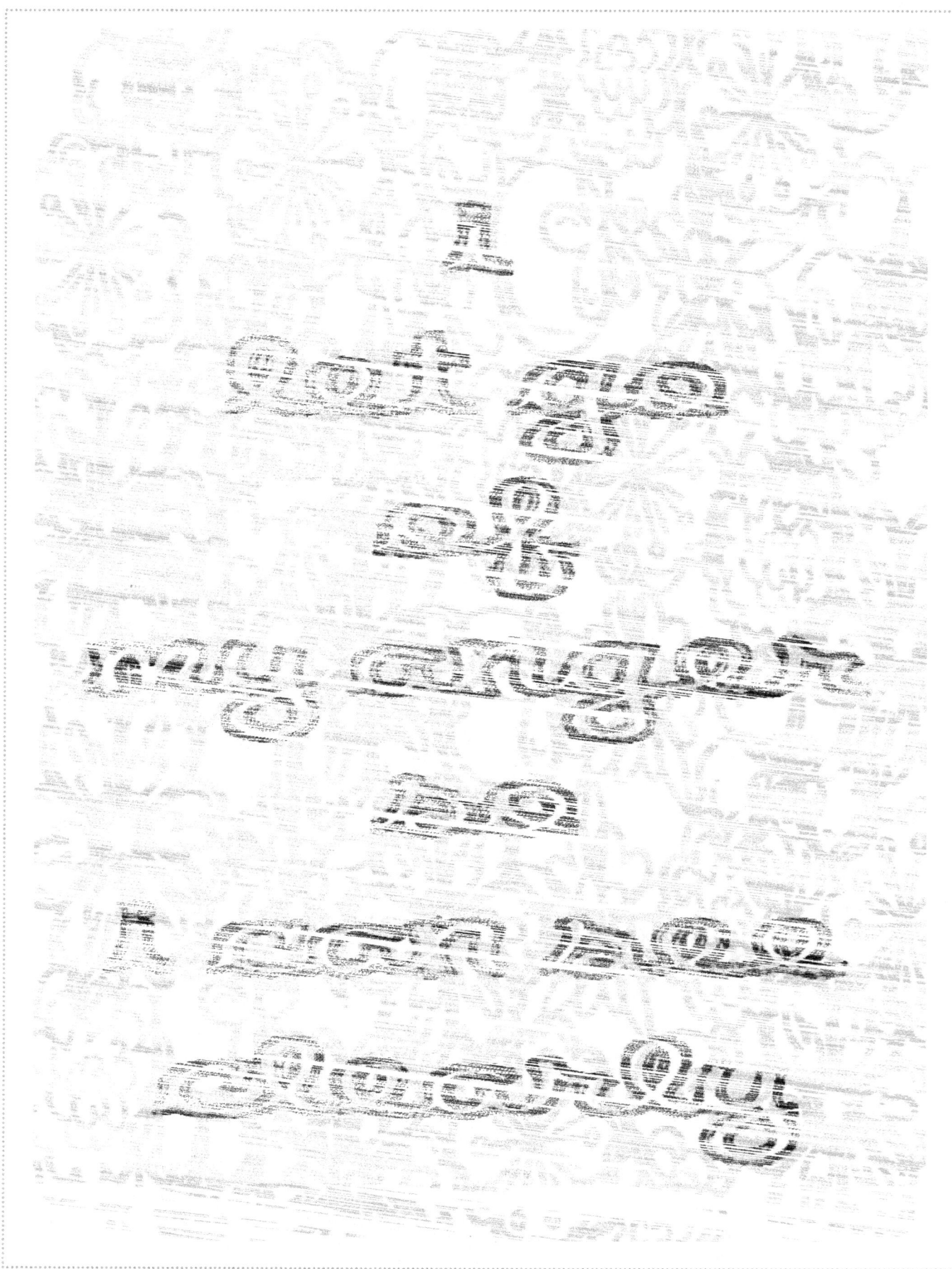

I
not go
of
my anger to
rock me
directly

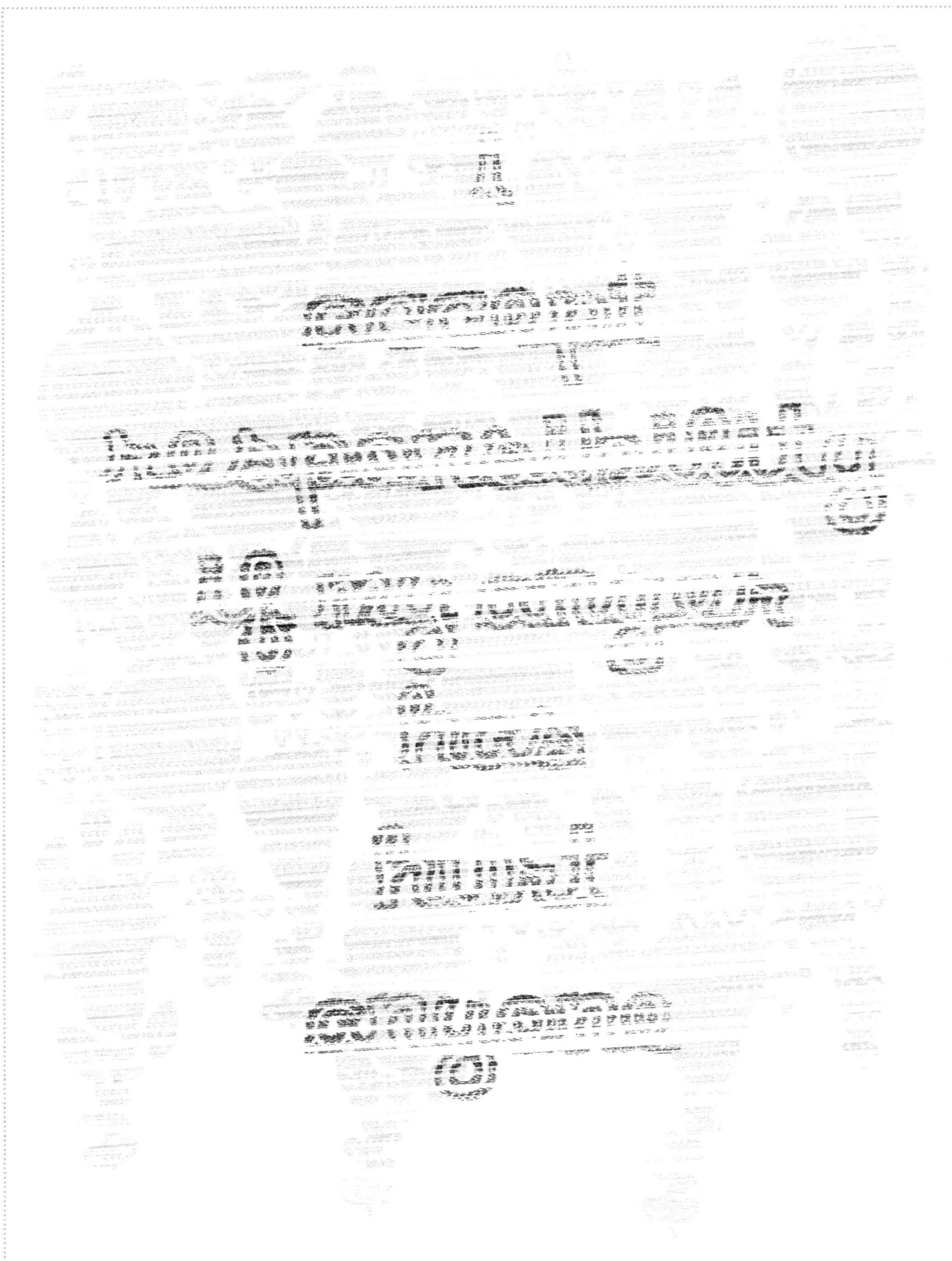

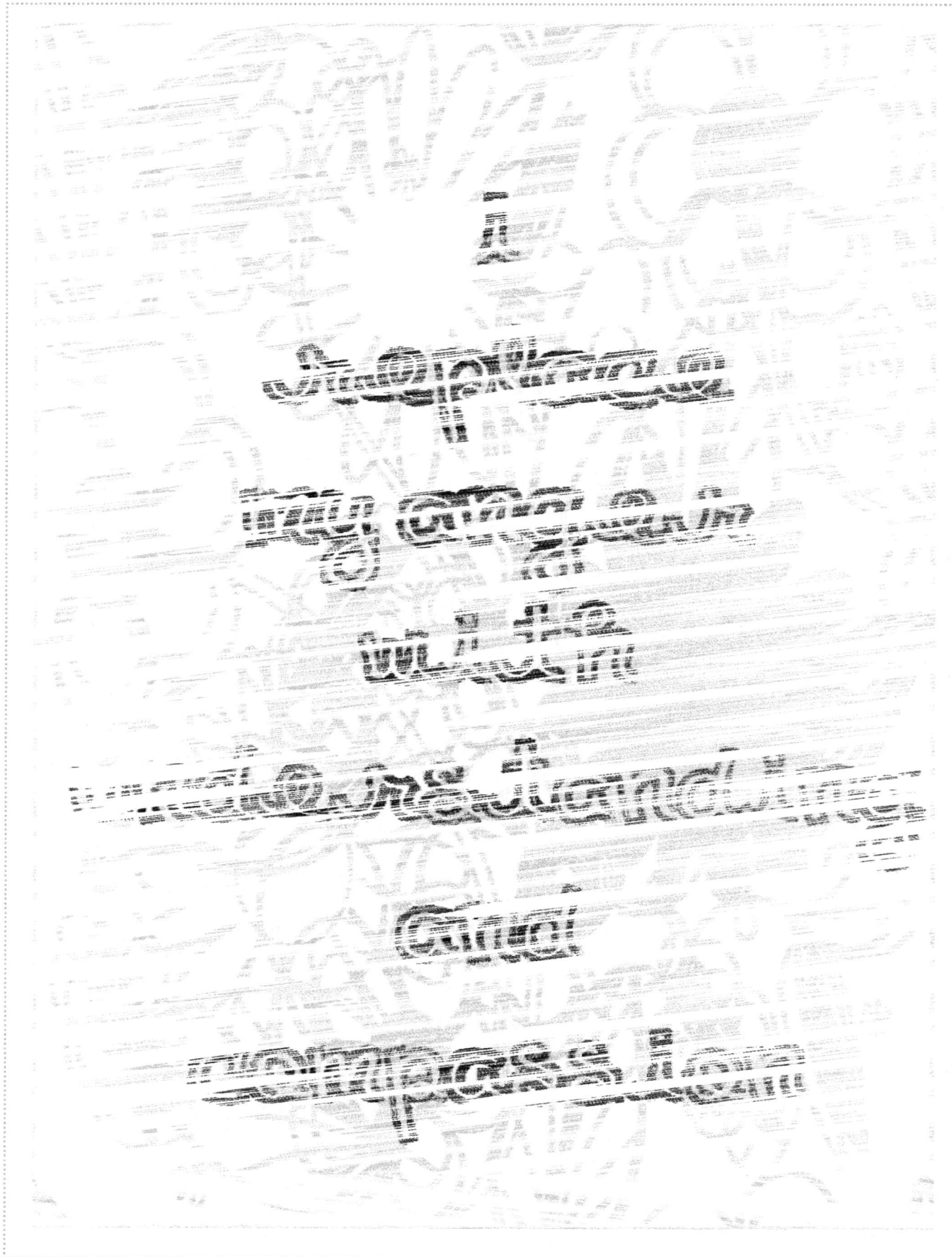

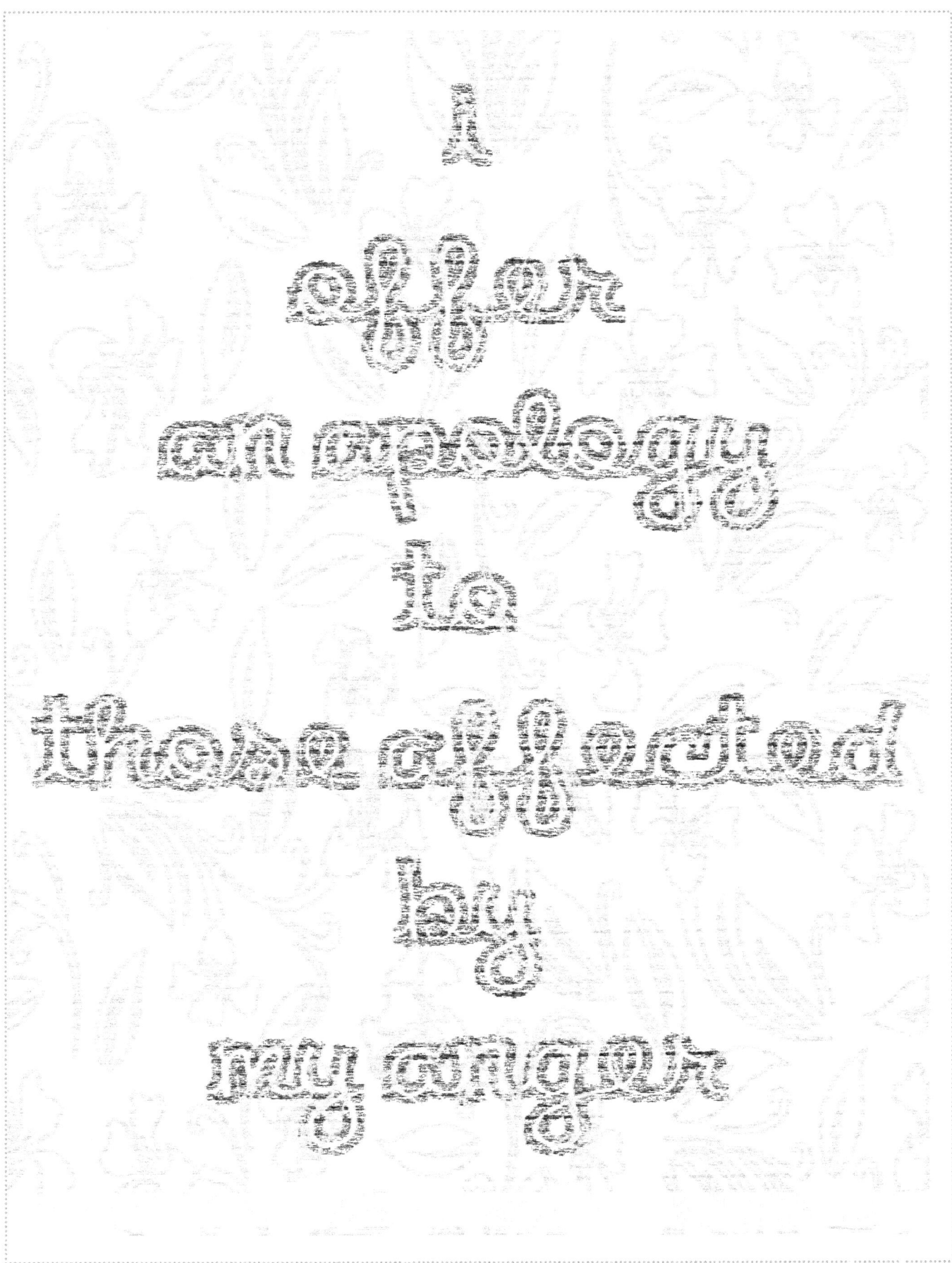

I offer an apology to those affected by my anger

6 WHEN YOU FEEL HOPELESS

the coloring page

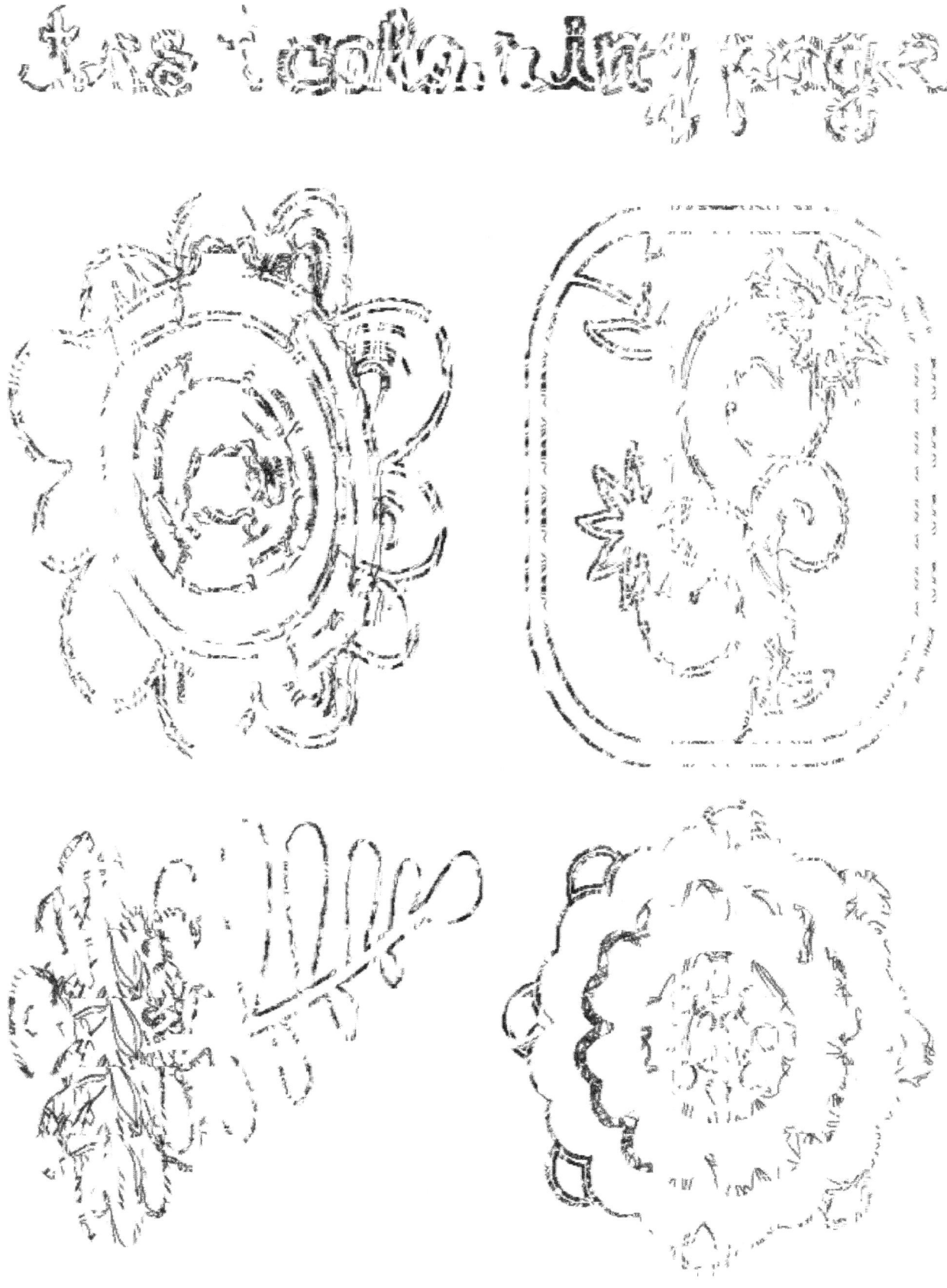

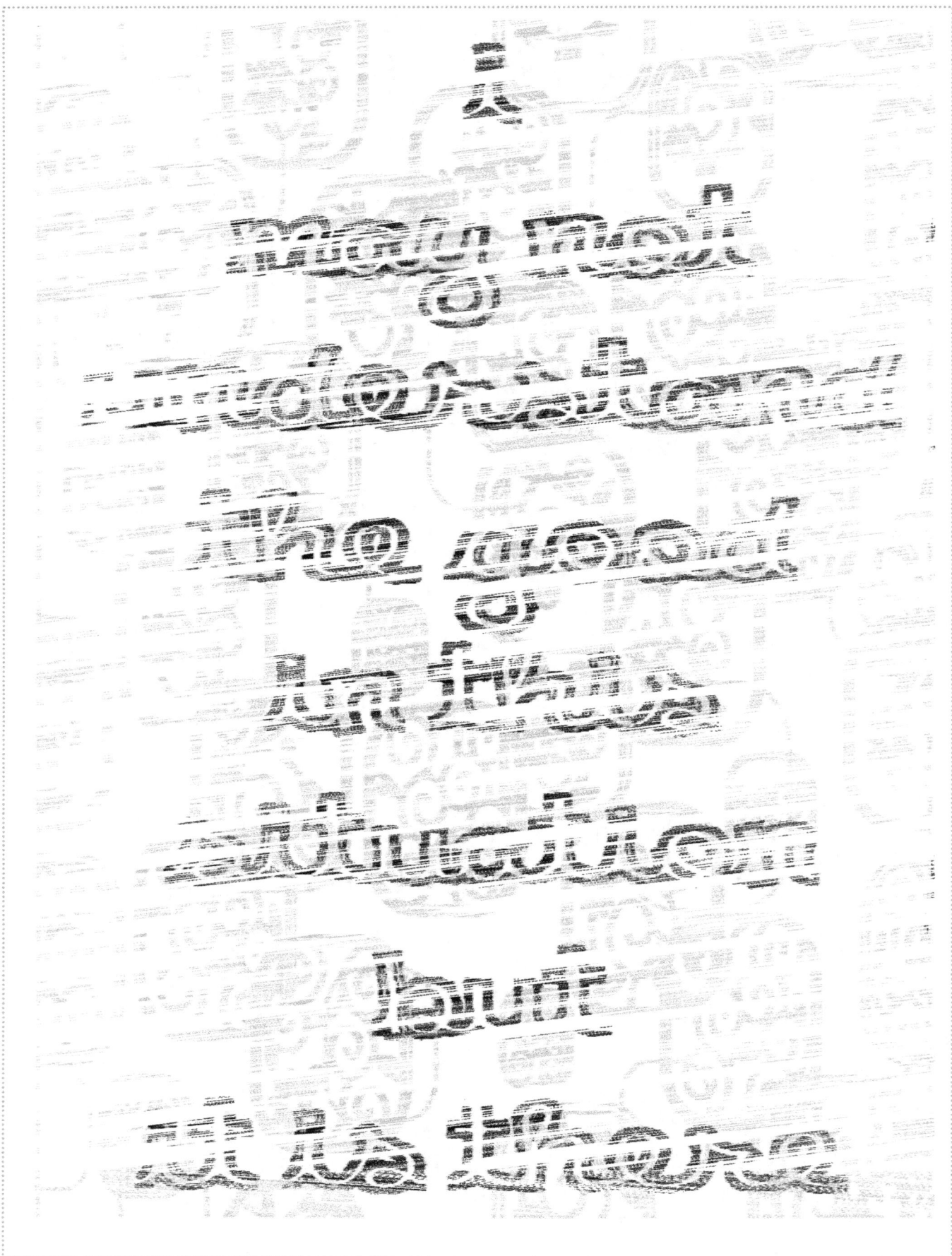

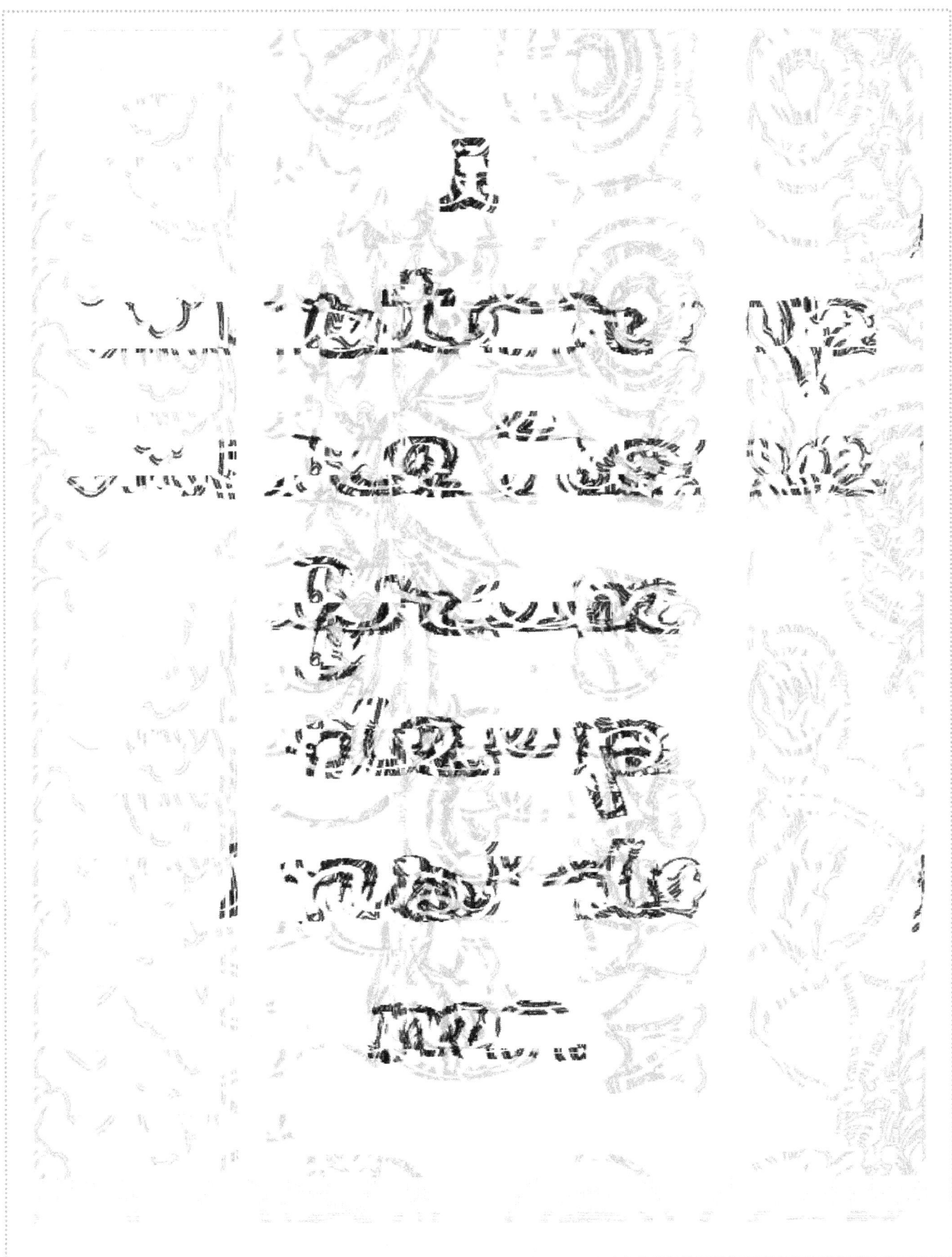

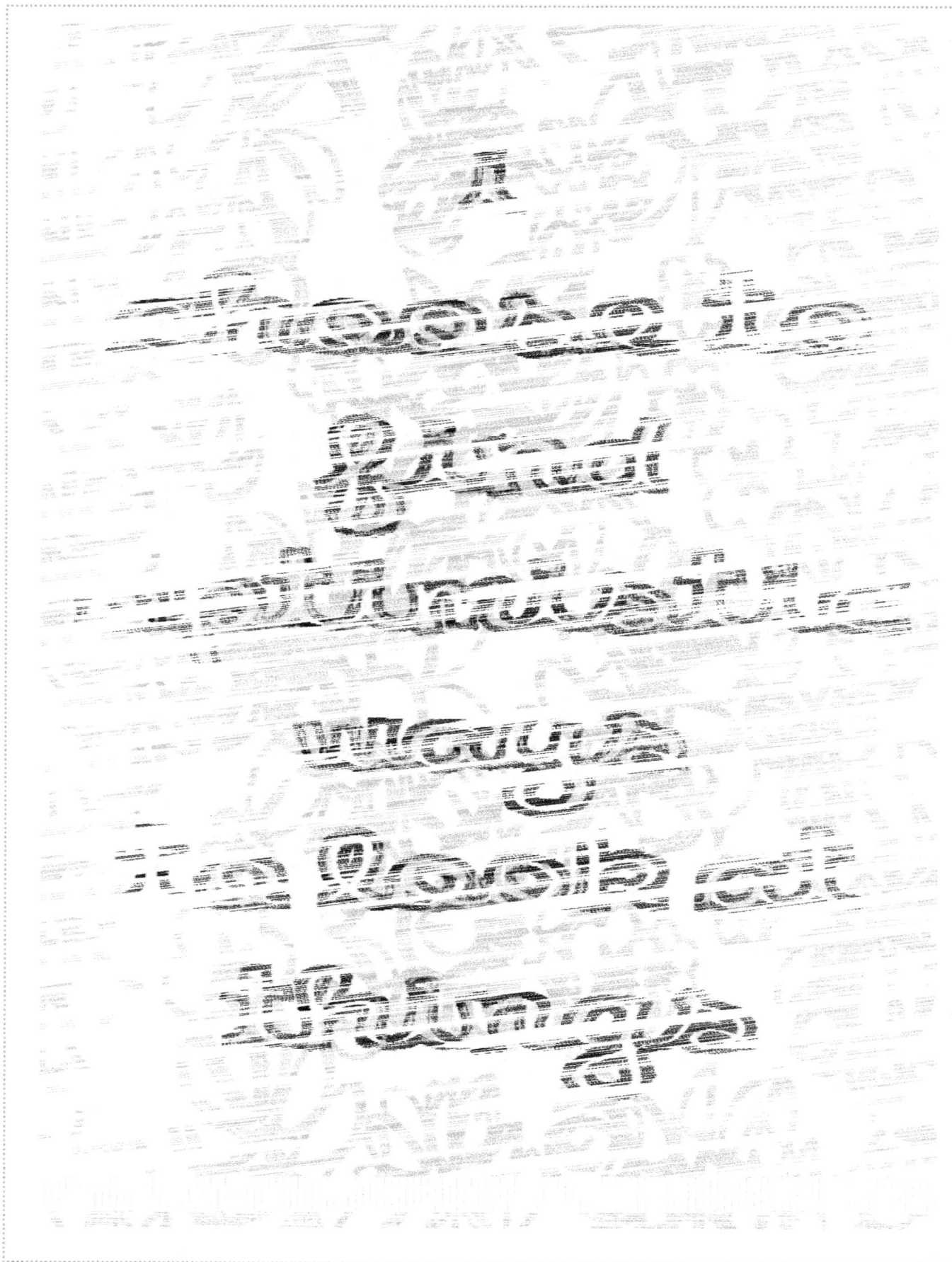

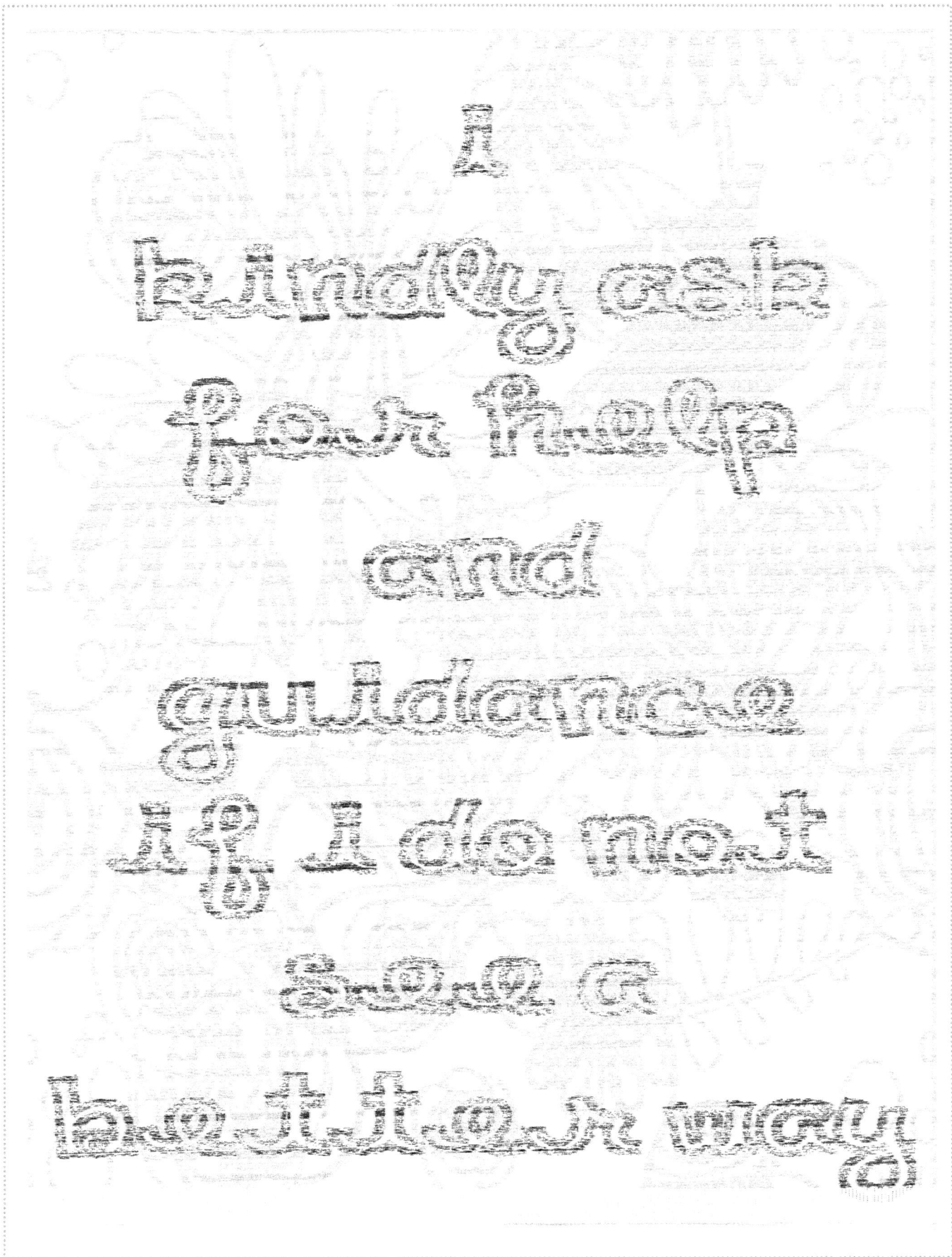

I kindly ask for help and guidance if I do not see a better way

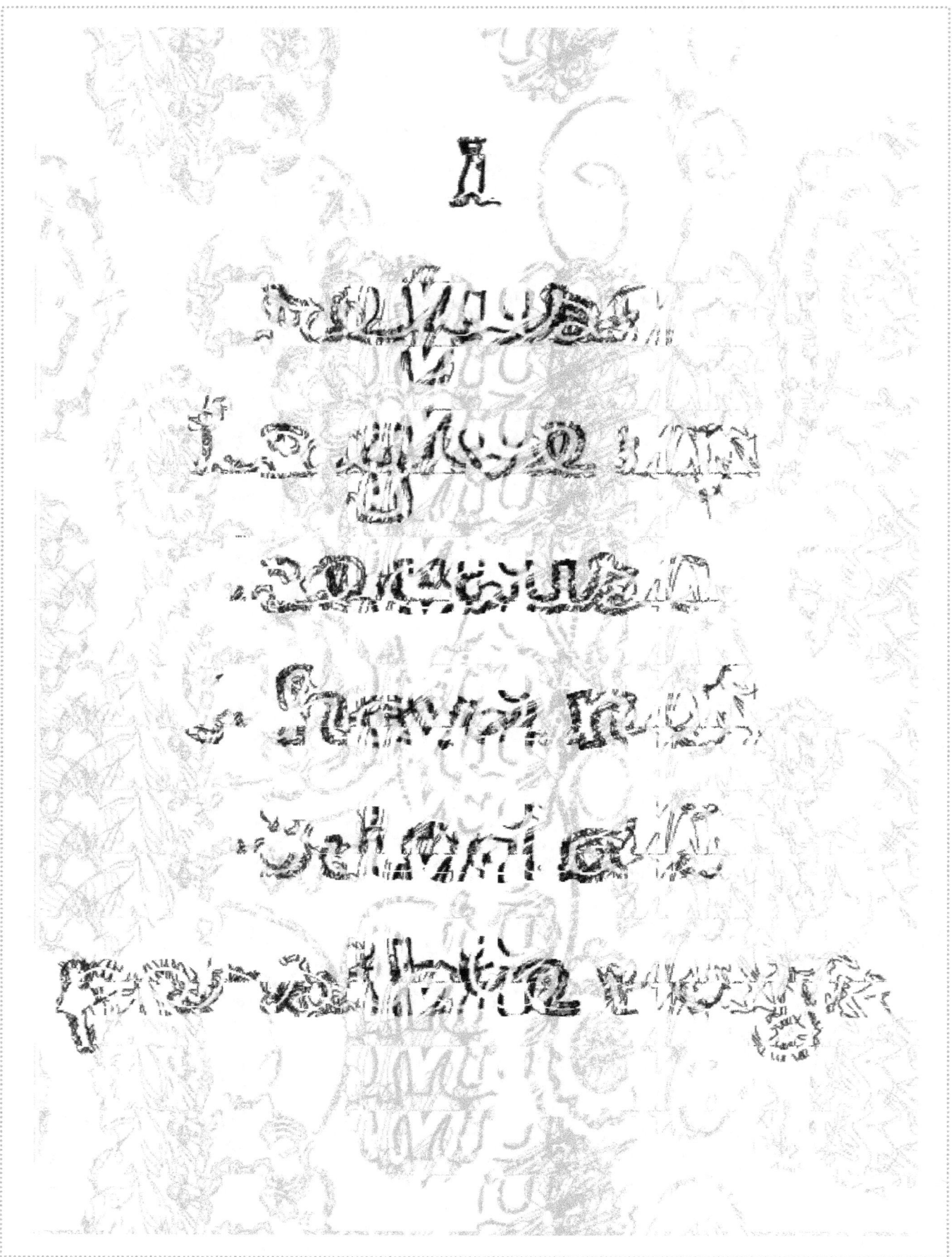

7 WHEN YOU FEEL CONFLICTED

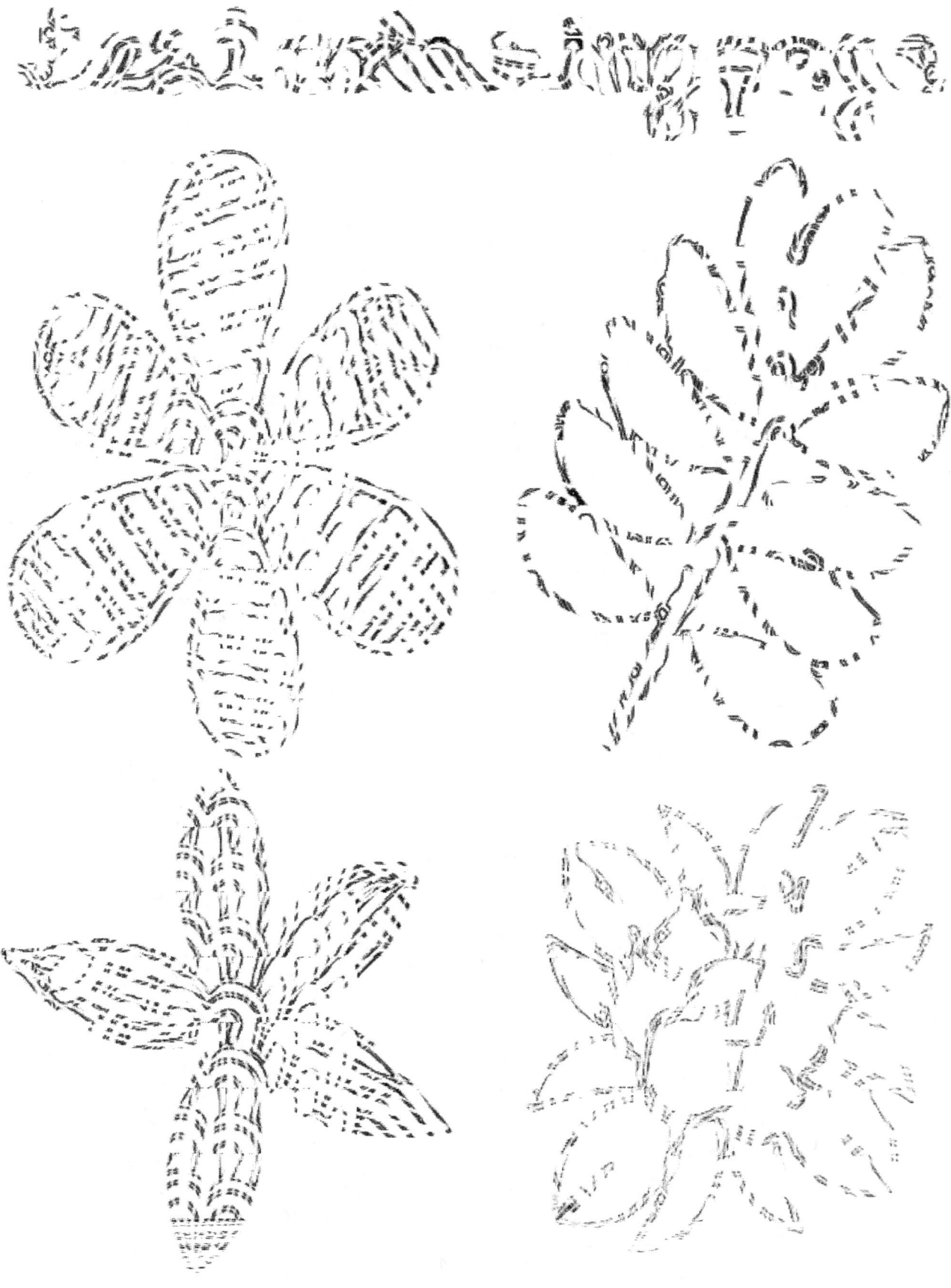

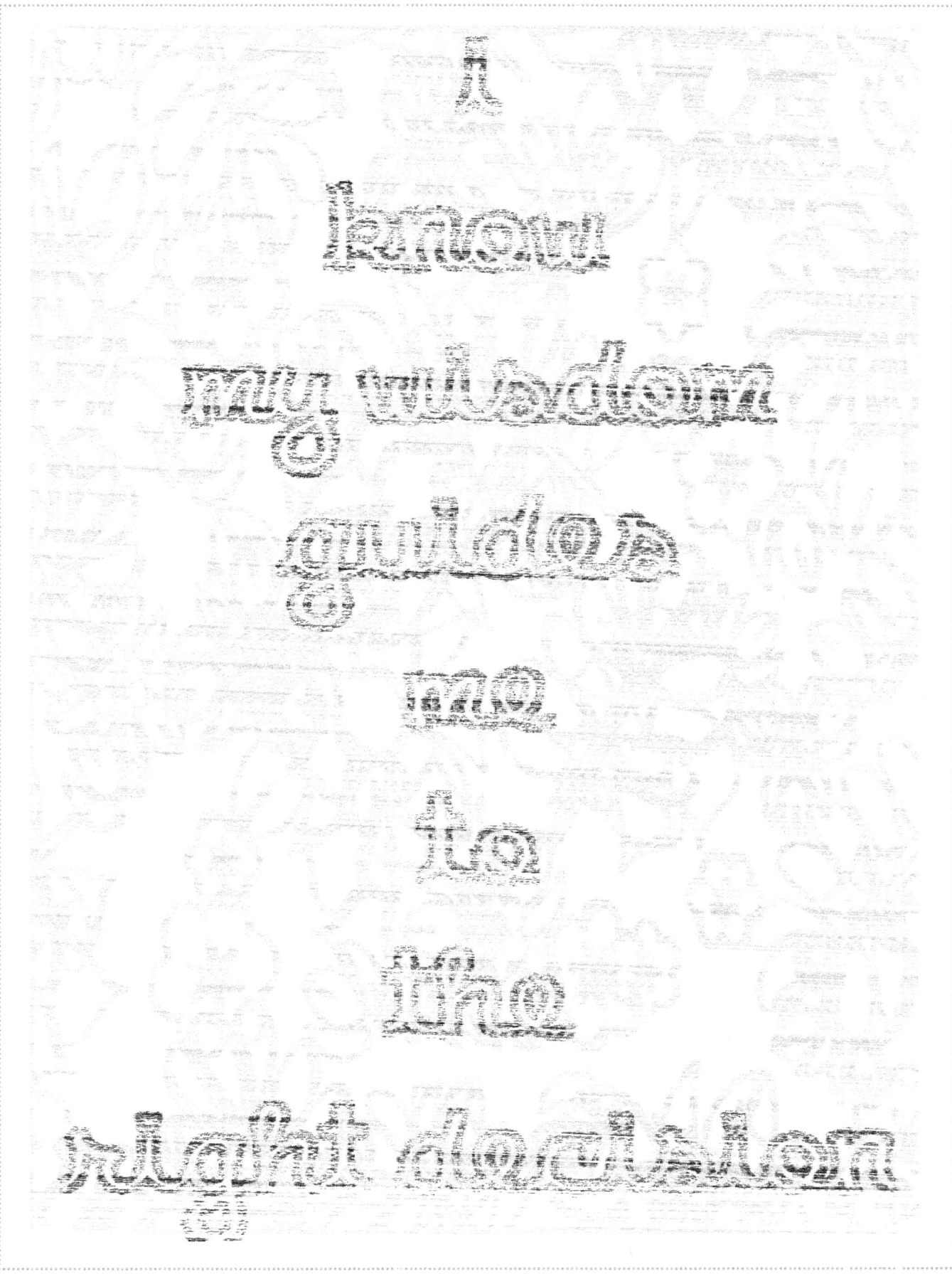

I know my wisdom guides me to the right decision

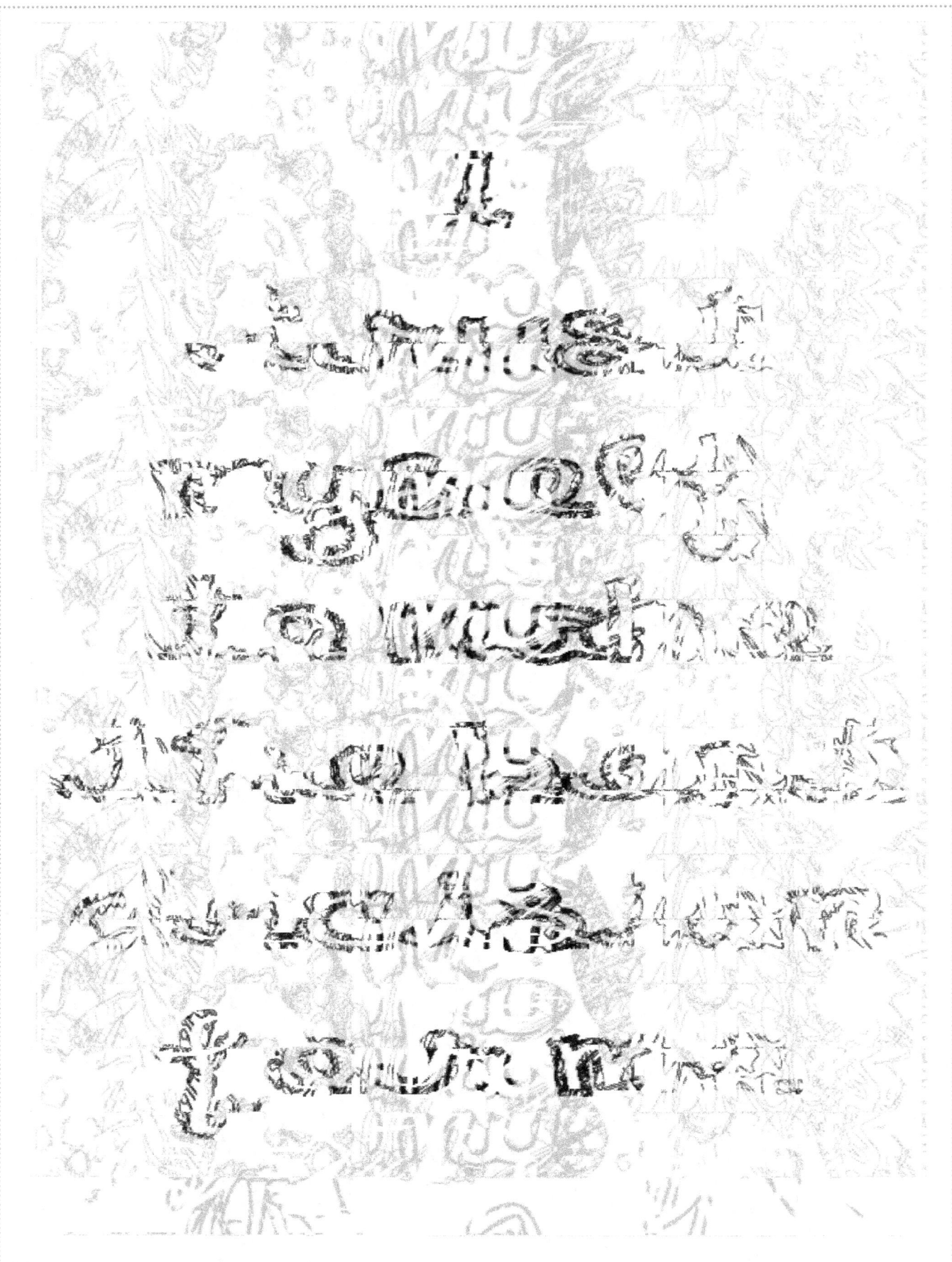

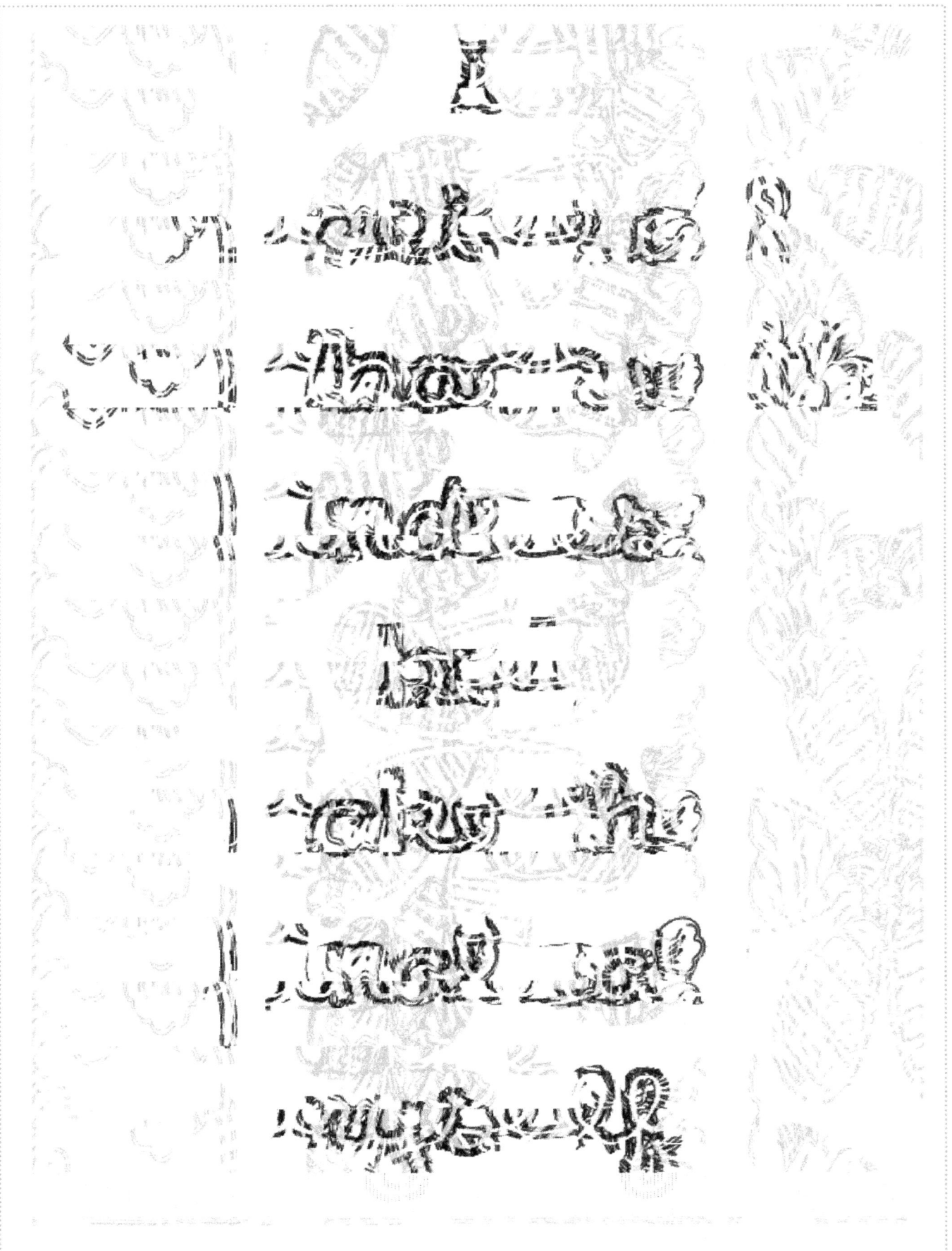

ACKNOWLEDGMENTS

It has been a depressing year to start of with especially with worries regarding the global economy and bombings hitting major cities in Europe and Asia To offset those anxieties, I took refuge in reading and have continuously sought out ways to calm my mind. A fad that caught on last year caught my eye and I found it a cathartic experience as I found myself coloring an adult coloring book as though as I was three year old.

While I found the act of coloring soothing, I was struck by the fact that a much more power subliminal message would permeate through if the act of coloring an image is done in tandem with affirmative words. Inspired by the classic book by Napoleon Hill's Think and Grow Rich and the more recent one by Rhonda Byrne's The Secret. I decided to map out a simple 30 day affirmations which would be embedded within the coloring book image to share with everyone. It would be useful for people who are intent on relaxing their mind, training the brain to focus and refining motor skills while releasing the creativity within themselves as they color the images in the best possible color combinations imaginable.

Thanks to Amazon and Createspace for making it possible for an author to self publish easily without the hassle of traditional publishing.

Thank you for purchasing this book. If you want to help me improve my next book, do visit booklaunch.io/willbraid and become part of the conversation.

NOTES

1 WHEN YOU FEEL LONELY OR SAD

1. HTTP://WWW.FREEPIK.COM/FREE-VECTOR/
2. HTTP://WWW.SUCAITIANXIA.COM/

2 WHEN YOU FEEL TERRIFIED

1. HTTP://WWW.FREEPIK.COM/FREE-VECTOR/
2. HTTP://WWW.SUCAITIANXIA.COM/

3 WHEN YOU FEEL INSIGNIFICANT

1. HTTP://WWW.FREEPIK.COM/FREE-VECTOR
2. HTTP://WWW.SUCAITIANXIA.COM/

4 WHEN YOU ARE NERVOUS OR AFRAID

1. HTTP://WWW.FREEPIK.COM/FREE-VECTOR/
2. HTTP://WWW.SUCAITIANXIA.COM/

5 WHEN YOU ARE ANGRY

1. HTTP://WWW.FREEPIK.COM/FREE-VECTOR/
2. HTTP://WWW.SUCAITIANXIA.COM/

6 WHEN YOU FEEL HOPELESS

1. HTTP://WWW.FREEPIK.COM/FREE-VECTOR/
2. HTTP://WWW.SUCAITIANXIA.COM/

7 WHEN YOU FEEL CONFLICTED

1. HTTP://WWW.FREEPIK.COM/FREE-VECTOR/
2. HTTP://WWW.SUCAITIANXIA.COM/

INDEX

affirmation   50
Afraid   25
Angry   31
conflicted   45
hopeless   38
insignificant   19
lonely   6
nervous   25
sad   6
terrified   12